NATIONAL GEOGRAPHIC

T0045273

Making a Hat

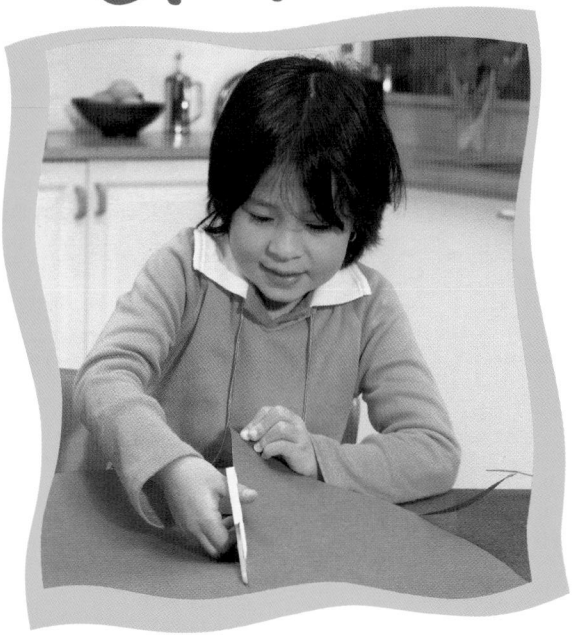

Kate McGough

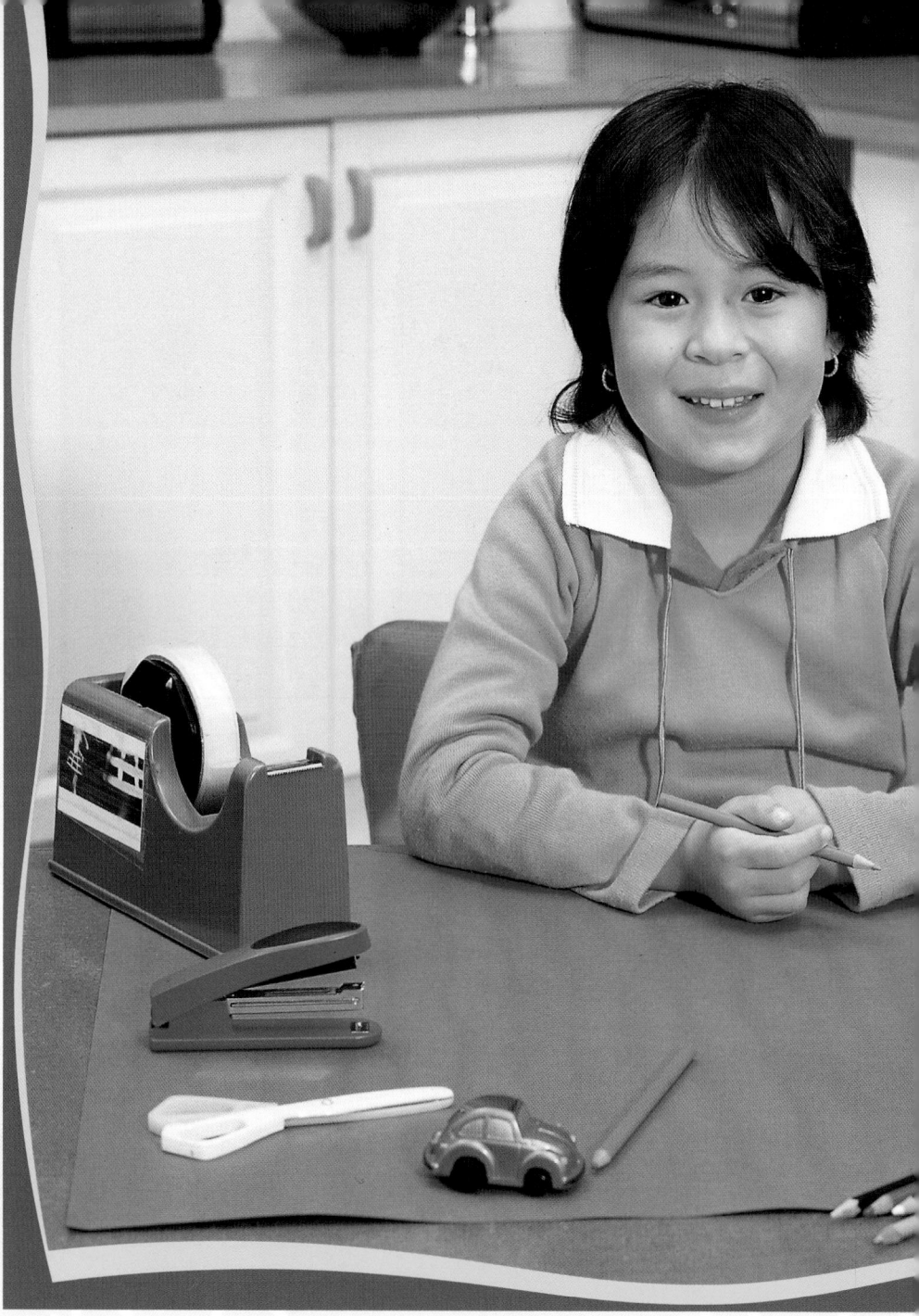

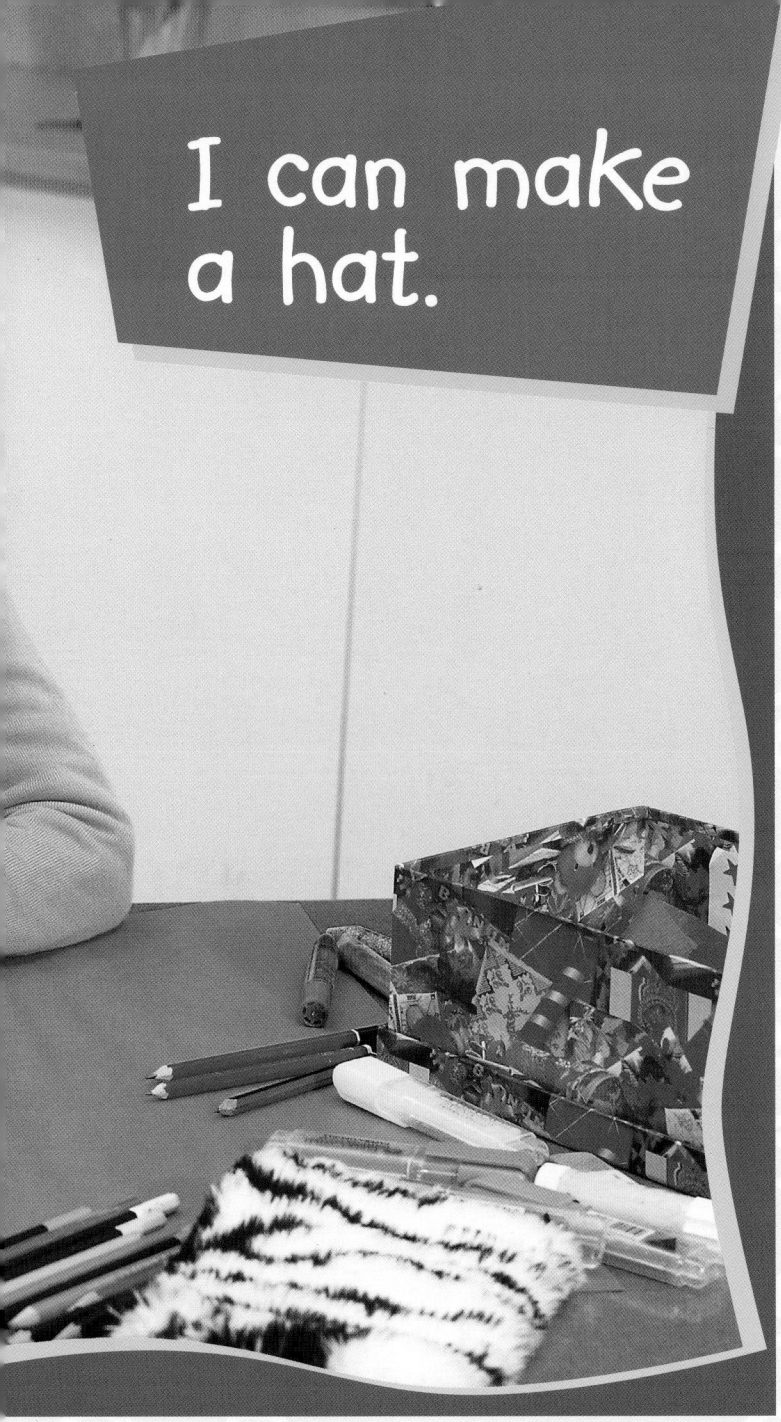

I can make
a hat.

I use scissors.

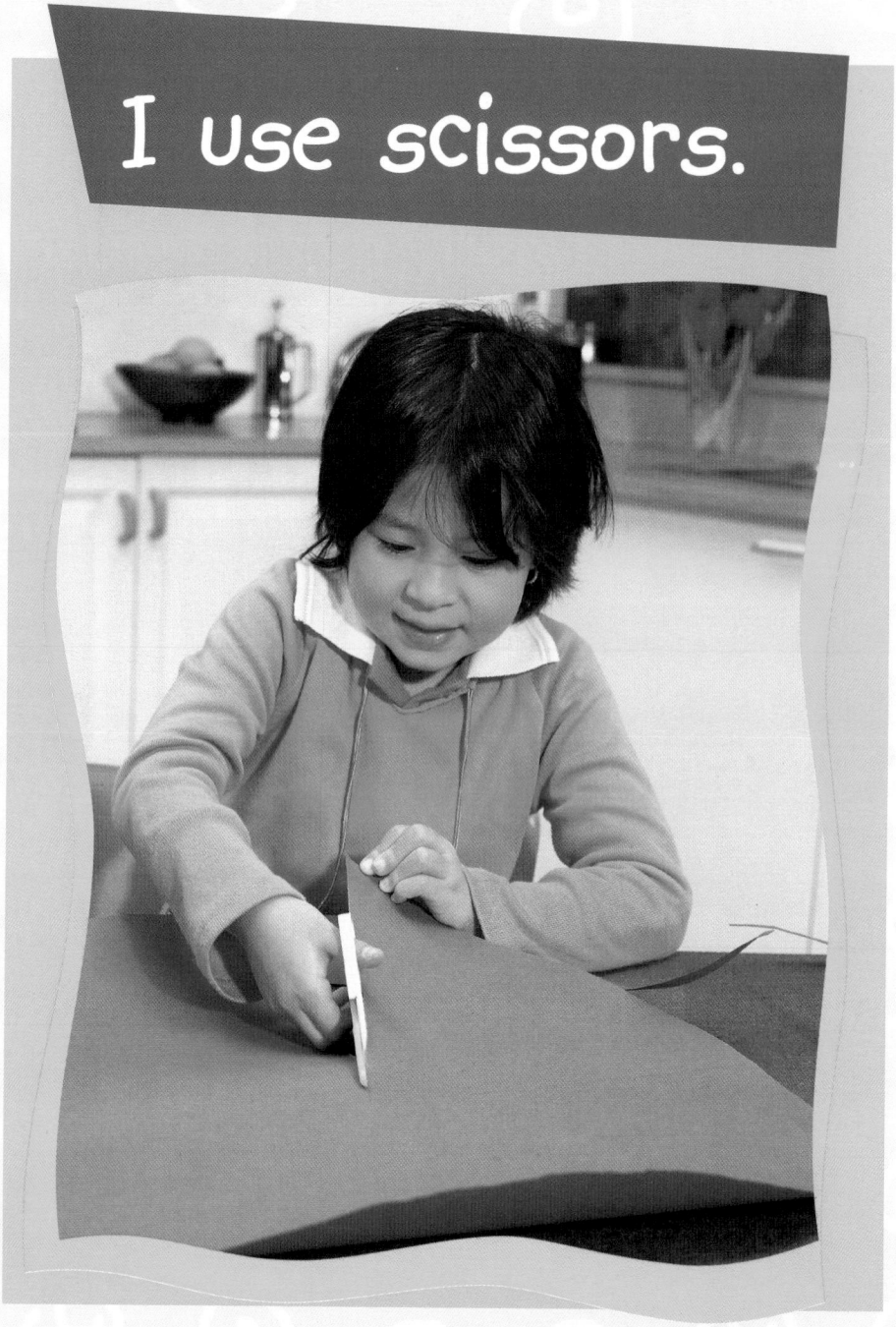

I use a stapler.

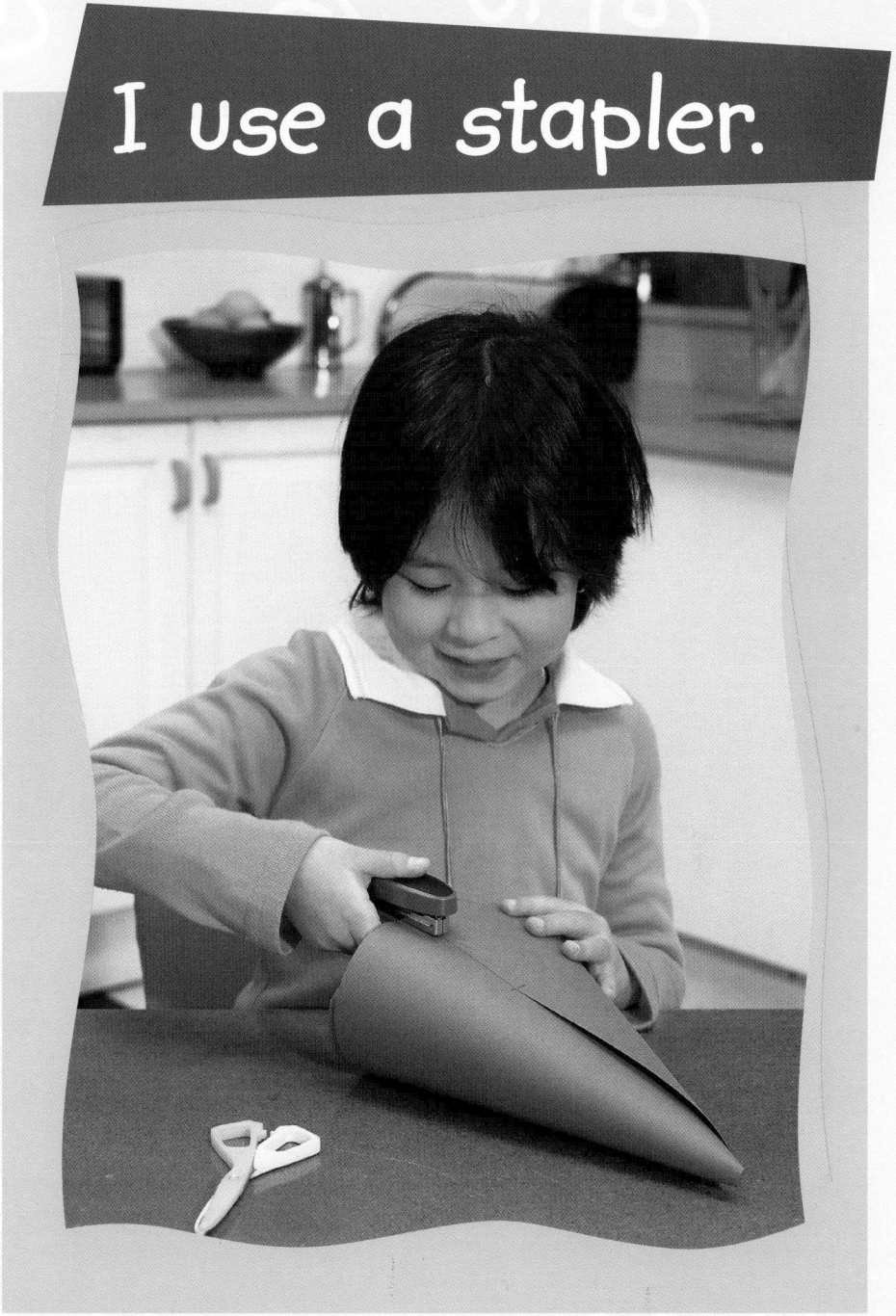

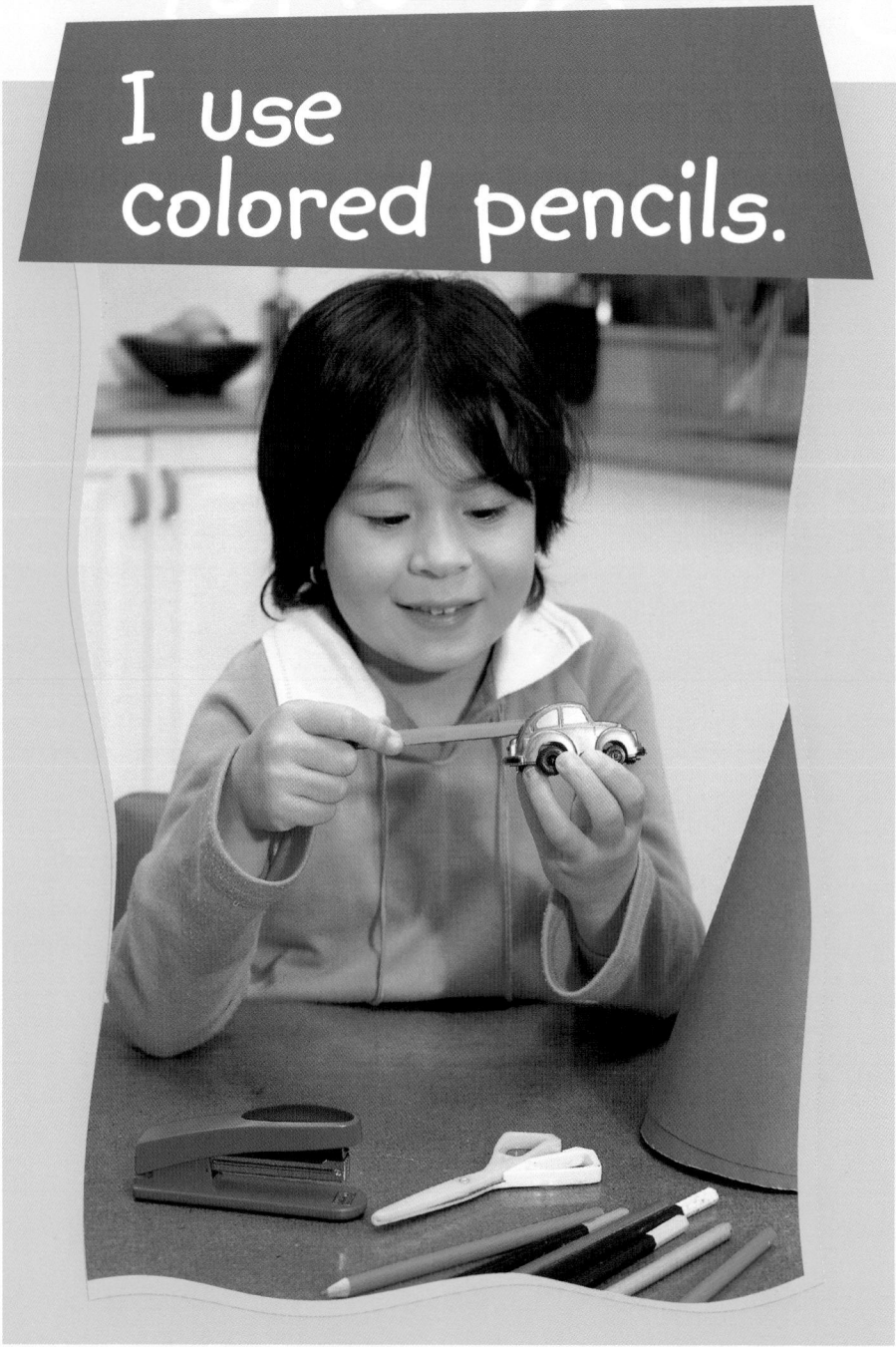
I use
colored pencils.

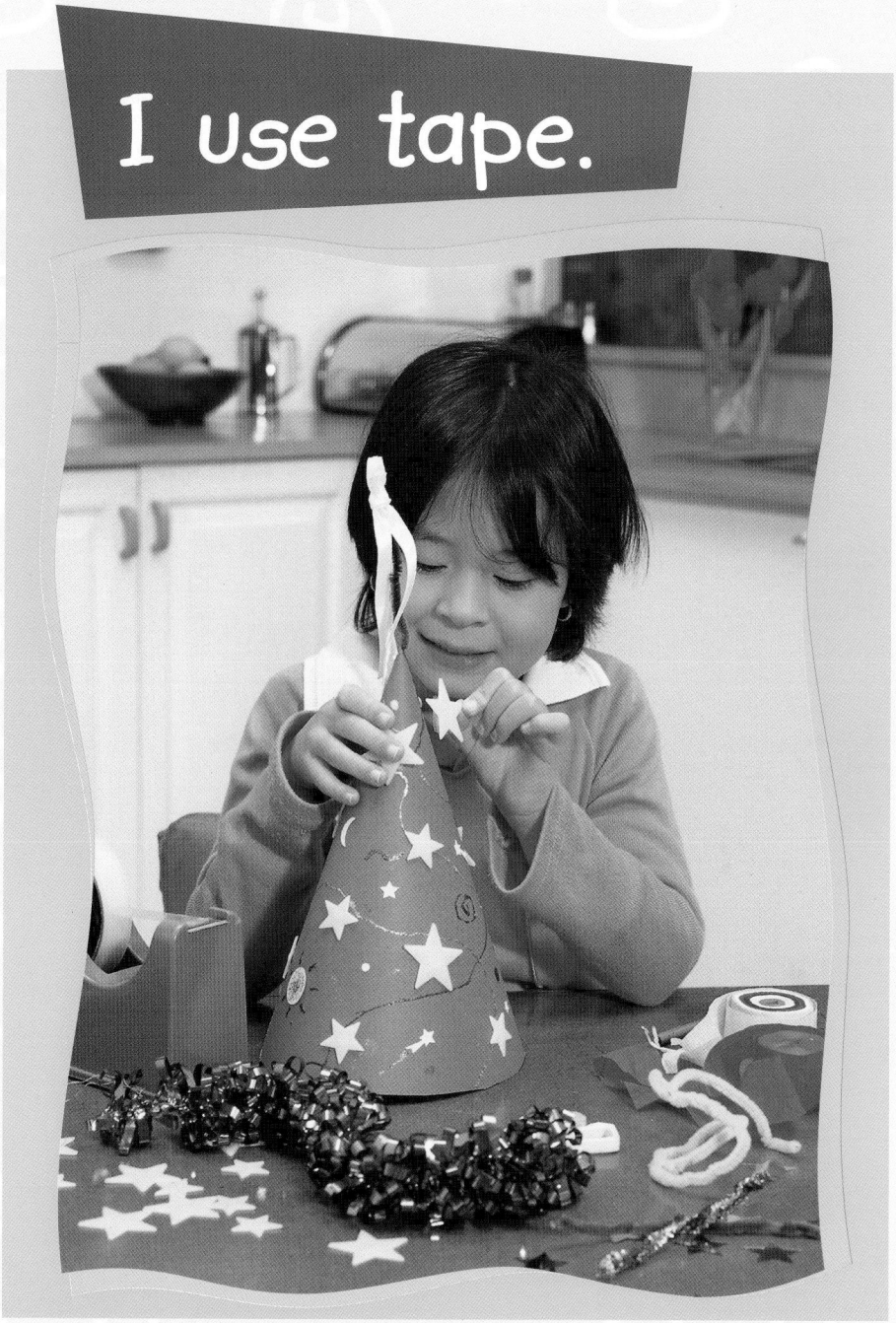
I use tape.

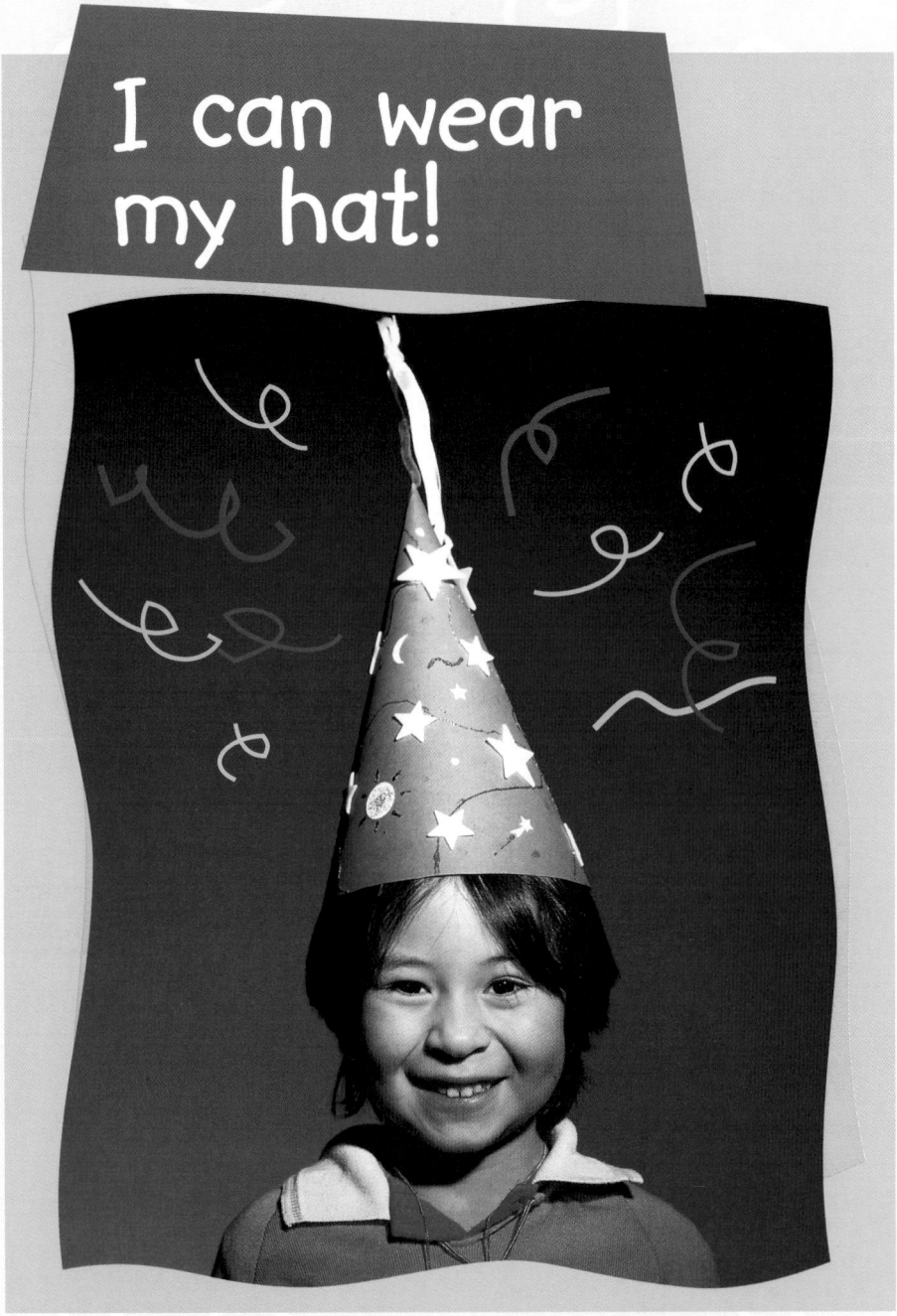
I can wear
my hat!